Mike J. Buchanan

TREES

every child should know

by Joe Maniscalco

Pacific Press Publishing Association

Mountain View, California   Omaha, Nebraska

REDWOOD

The redwood is a giant tree. It grows more than 300 feet tall. Redwoods are among the oldest living things in the world. Some of these trees are more than 3,000 years old.

Redwoods grow in California. There are two kinds of redwoods. One kind grows near the seacoast, and the other kind grows high in the mountains.

These trees have a thick reddish-brown bark that is very soft. Insects do not like to eat holes in redwoods, because the wood has a juice called tannin. Forest fires cannot burn the thick bark very well, either. That's why redwoods live so long.

CHESTNUT

Did you know that the chestnut tree is related to the oak trees? Most chestnut trees grow in the eastern part of America, but they have been planted in other places, too.

The leaves of the chestnut are long, and they have sharp points like needles. Their nuts are very big. There are two nuts in each pod. The pods are covered with long, sharp needles.

Chestnuts taste good after they have been roasted over a fire. Animals and birds like them for food, too.

Chestnut trees sometimes grow to be 100 feet tall.

ASPEN

Aspen trees grow in high mountains. There are different kinds of aspens. The kind shown on this page is called the quaking aspen.

Quaking means shaking. The leaves of these trees are thin and almost round. When the wind blows, the leaves shake, and that is where the trees get their name.

Beavers like to chew soft, white aspen wood. They also make their dams and homes from the wood of aspen trees.

Aspens grow in groves, and often near lakes and streams. In the fall their leaves turn bright yellow.

EUCALYPTUS

To say the name of this tree, say "you-ka-lip-tus."

Tall eucalyptus trees grow side by side in groves. Together they act like curtains to keep out the strong wind.

Eucalyptus trees have long leaves that are very oily. The bark falls off the trees, and hangs in long pieces. Under the peeled-off bark, the trees are white and smooth.

In Australia little koala bears live in eucalyptus trees. Koala bears eat eucalyptus leaves for breakfast, for dinner, and for supper. When they have finished eating the leaves from one tree, they jump to another tree and eat some more.

DOUGLAS FIR

Next to the giant redwood trees, the Douglas fir is the biggest tree. Some full-grown Douglas firs are more than 200 feet tall.

The cones from these trees have round scales, and toothlike growths on the scales. Their leaves are something like pine needles, and are short and flat. The needles grow around each twig like stripes on a candy cane.

Douglas fir trees grow best where it is cold and wet. The trunks are straight, and round, and strong. People use more Douglas-fir wood than any other kind of wood for building houses.

BLACK OAK

The California black oak has a gray, rough trunk, with big, heavy limbs. The leaves are a dark green color on top, and a light green underneath. When autumn comes the leaves turn yellow and brown.

The black-oak tree has big acorns. They are about one and one-half inches long. Many different kinds of animals and birds eat the acorns in the fall and winter.

Indians used to eat acorns, too. The Indians pounded acorns into flour. They used the flour for baking acorn cakes.

SPRUCE

Norway spruce trees grow in the coldest parts of the country. The trees have big, long cones. The needles of the spruce tree have four sides, and they have sharp points.

When this tree is young, it is stiff, and stands up straight. When it grows older, the branches grow heavy and hang down. Birds and animals eat the tender needles. Deer like to eat the twigs when the twigs are green and tender.

Spruce trees make good lumber. The wood is soft, but strong.

BIRCH

There are many kinds of birch trees. The one in this picture is called a paper birch. Some people call it a white birch, and other people call it a canoe birch. Indians used to make canoes from birch bark. They used this bark to make dishes and baskets, too.

Sometimes the paper-birch tree grows to be 100 feet tall. Its bark is smooth and white, with dark lines running through it. The bark of old trees becomes scaly.

Birch leaves have jagged edges that look like little teeth. The leaves are green in summer, but in autumn they turn bright yellow.

POPLAR

This poplar tree is called a Lombardy poplar. Many of these trees grow in the country of Italy, and now there are many in the United States, too.

Lombardy poplars are tall, thin trees. Many times people plant them in long rows. They look almost like a line of marching soldiers.

The leaves of these trees are green in the summer, but they turn bright yellow in the fall. When the wind blows them off, they scatter like golden snowflakes. It is a pretty sight to see.

NORWAY MAPLE

Can you guess where the Norway maple first came from? You are right, if you guessed the country of Norway. Today there are many of these trees in our own country.

The leaves of Norway-maple trees look something like the leaves growing on sugar maples. But the sugar-maple leaves are not so wide.

In the fall the leaves turn bright yellow. When you see these trees far away, with the sun shining on them, you might think they are made of gold.

SUGAR MAPLE

The sugar-maple tree grows in the eastern part of our country. Maple sugar and syrup are made from its sweet juice.

The sugar maple is beautiful, too. Most of its leaves turn deep red in the autumn, but some of them turn bright orange or yellow. As winter comes, the leaves fall to the ground and turn to a brown color.

Children like to play in the fallen leaves. Pet animals like to play in the leaves, too.

PIÑON PINE

There are many kinds of pine trees. One of them is called the piñon pine. Piñon is pronounced "peen-yone."

Piñon pines are found in the western part of this country. They usually grow in dry places. They do not need very much water.

These pine trees have short, stiff needles, that come in bunches of twos and threes.

Pine trees, and some other kinds of trees, too, are called conifers. This means that they have cones. Piñon-pine cones have seeds that are called pine nuts. Pine nuts are delicious to eat. Indians like to eat the nuts.